Chelipeds *(Make 2)*

In BC1, CO 37 sts. Continue, working back and forth in rows as follows:

Row 1 (wrong side): Sl1 kwise, P12, w&t.

Row 2: K11, w&t.

Row 3: P10, w&t.

Row 4: K9, w&t.

Row 5: P8, w&t.

Row 6: K7, w&t.

Row 7: P19, w&t.

Row 8: K9, w&t.

Row 9: P8, w&t.

Row 10: K7, w&t.

Row 11: P6, w&t.

Row 12: K5, w&t.

Row 13: P21.

Row 14: Sl1 kwise, K12, w&t.

Row 15: P13.

Row 16: Sl1 kwise, K11, w&t.

Row 17: P12.

Row 18: Sl1 kwise, K10, w&t.

Row 19: P11.

Row 20: Sl1 kwise, K9, w&t.

Row 21: P10.

Row 22: Sl1 kwise, P35, K1.

BO all sts as follows: *P2tog, transfer st back to left needle, continue from * until only 1 st remains. Cut yarn, thread through final st, and pull tight.

Using BC1, whip st the first 4 sts from the CO edge to the first 4 sts of the BO edge.

Next, use BC2 and pick up 32 sts from the BO edge of the work. Turn work. Continue along CO edge and pick up another 32 sts using BC2. See **Figure 1** for guidance.

Figure 1

Figure 2

Cut BC2 yarn, leaving a long tail. Using a tapestry needle and this yarn tail, graft (Kitchener st) the sts picked up from the CO edge to the sts picked up from the BO edge. While you are grafting, lightly stuff the cheliped with fiberfill.

If desired, place a folded chenille stem inside the cheliped while you are stuffing and grafting. This will allow you to pose the chelipeds of your finished creature.

To work the pincer of the cheliped, use BC1 yarn, and pick up 6 sts from the side of the cheliped. Turn the work, and pick up another 6 sts from the opposite side of the cheliped, for a total of 12 sts. You will be picking up the sts close to the tip of the cheliped near the intersection of the first and second segments. Use **Figure 2** for guidance.

Continue, working in rounds, as follows:

Round 1: K4, K2tog, SSK, K4—10 sts.

Round 2: K1, M1L, K2, K2tog, SSK, K2, M1R, K1—10 sts.

Round 3: K3, K2tog, SSK, K3—8 sts.

Round 4: K1, M1L, K1, K2tog, SSK, K1, M1R, K1—8 sts.

Round 5: K2, K2tog, SSK, K2—6 sts.

Lightly stuff the pincer with fiberfill.

Round 6: K1, M1L, K2tog, SSK, M1R, K1—6 sts.

Round 7: K1, K2tog, SSK, K1—4 sts.

Cut yarn, thread through final 4 sts and pull tight.

Legs (Make 4)

In BC1, CO 31 sts. Continue, working in rows, as follows:

Row 1 (wrong side): Sl1 kwise, P9, w&t.

Row 2: K7, w&t.

Row 3: P6, w&t.

Row 4: K4, w&t.

Row 5: P15, w&t.

Row 6: K9, w&t.

Row 7: P8, w&t.

Row 8: K7, w&t.

Row 9: P6, w&t.

Row 10: K5, w&t.

Row 11: P18.

Row 12: Sl1 kwise, K9, w&t.

Row 13: P10.

Row 14: Sl1 kwise, K8, w&t.

Row 15: P9.

Row 16: Sl1 kwise, K7, w&t.

Row 17: P8.

Row 18: Sl1 kwise, K6, w&t.

Row 19: P7.

Row 20: Sl1 kwise, P29, K1.

BO sts as follows: *P2tog, transfer st to left needle, repeat from * until only 1 lp remains. Cut yarn, thread through final st, and pull tight. Using BC1, whip st the first 10 sts of the cast-on edge to the BO edge. Now, use BC2 to pick up 20 sts from the CO edge. Continuing with the same yarn, pick up another 20 sts from the BO edge, for a total of 40 sts. Pick up these sts from the lps just inside of the CO or BO edge. This will create a clean demarcation between the carapace of the limb and its underside. Your leg should now resemble **Figure 3**.

Figure 3

Divide these 40 sts evenly onto 2 needles. Cut yarn, leaving a long tail. Using a tapestry needle and this long tail, graft (Kitchener st) the sts from the first needle to the sts on the second needle. While doing this, lightly stuff the leg. For a pose-able leg, fold a chenille stem in half and twist securely. Insert this, blunt end first, into the leg, and stuff fiberfill around this as you are grafting.

Assembly of Legs

Using **Figure 4** for guidance, sew the four legs into the open end of the shell. Using **Figure 5** for guidance, sew the two chelipeds into the open end of the shell, allowing them to rest atop the legs.

Figure 4

Figure 5

Head

CO 25 sts in BC1. Join these sts into a round and continue:

Rounds 1–3: Knit.

Round 4: SSK, K11, K2tog, SSK, K6, K2tog—21 sts.

Round 5: Knit.

Round 6: SSK, K9, K2tog, SSK, K4, K2tog—17 sts.

Round 7: Knit.

Round 8: SSK, K2, Sl2-K1-P2SSO, K2, K2tog, SSK, K2, K2tog—11 sts.

Round 9: Knit.

Round 10: SSK, Sl2-K1-P2SSO, K2tog, SSK, K2tog—5 sts.

Rounds 11 & 12: Knit.

Round 13: Sl2-K1-P2SSO, K2—3 sts.

Cut yarn, thread through final 3 sts and pull tight.

Whiskers

Work the base of the left whisker as follows. Using BC1, pick up 4 sts on the decrease line on the left side of the head. To pick these sts up, start near the pointed tip of the face, and pick up one st on every row, working along the decrease line. Turn the work, and pick up another 4 sts on the decrease line behind the first 4 sts. Use **Figure 6** for guidance in picking up these 8 sts. Join these stitches in a round and proceed:

Figure 6

Round 1: Knit.

Round 2: K2, K2tog, SSK, K2—6 sts.

Round 3: K1, K2tog, SSK, 1—4 sts.

Round 4: K2tog, SSK—2 sts.

Cut yarn, leaving a 3" (7.5 cm) tail. Thread this yarn tail through the remaining 2 sts and pull tight. Using your tapestry needle, break apart the plies of this yarn to create the whiskers on the left side of the face.

Work the base of the right whisker analogously by picking up sts on the right side of the head.

Eyestalks

Work the left eyestalk as follows. Pick up 3 sts on the top of the left side of the head as shown in **Figure 7**. Note that the sts are picked up in a ring on the left side of the head, very close to the tip of the snout.

Figure 7

Join these sts into a round and proceed:

Rounds 1–7: Knit.

Round 8: K-fb 3 times—6 sts.

Rounds 9 & 10: Knit.

Cut BC1 yarn, and attach EC yarn. Continue:

Rounds 11–13: Knit.

Cut yarn, thread through remaining 6 sts, and pull tight.

Work the right eyestalk analogously by picking up sts on the right side of the head.

Final Assembly and Finishing

Stuff the head with fiberfill. Sew the head into the opening of the shell, above the legs and chelipeds. Be sure to sew the CO edge of the head to the inside of the lip of the shell. This will give the illusion that your little crab is peeking out of his shell. Before you finish sewing, be sure that you have adequately stuffed your creation. Take care of any loose yarn ends.

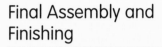

Common Octopus

Octopuses are among my favorite invertebrates. This knit version is a real tactile treat. Not only is it soft and huggable, but the arms can be made pose-able by the use of chenille stems, making for hours of cephalopod-filled fun!

yarn

Worsted weight
MC (red): 75 yd (68.5 m)
CC (yellow): 25 yd (23 m)
Small amounts of natural white and dark brown for embroidering eyes

needles

• One set U.S. size 5 (3.75 mm) double-pointed needles
and/or
• Two U.S. size 5 (3.75 mm) circular needles, 24" (61 cm) long

notions

• Eight 12" (30.5 cm) chenille stems
• Fiberfill stuffing
• Tapestry needle

gauge

22 to 24 sts = 4" (10 cm) in stockinette stitch

dimensions

Diameter: 7" (18 cm)
Height: 4" (10 cm)
Mantle length: 5" (12.5 cm)

difficulty

Intermediate/Experienced

Pattern

Tentacles *(Make 8)*

In CC, CO 28 sts.

Switch to MC.

Row 1 (Right side): K28.

Row 2: P14, w&t.

Row 3: K14.

Row 4: P21, w&t.

Row 5: K21.

Row 6: P7, w&t.

Row 7: K7.

Row 8: P28.

Switch to back to CC.

Row 9: K28.

BO all sts. Leave a long tail of yarn and thread through lp. Pull tight.

Use tapestry needle and whip st CO edge to BO edge with long tail of yarn.

Mantle and Head

CO 4 sts in MC. Divide onto 4 dpns or 2 circular needles. Join into a round.

Round 1: Knit.

Round 2: *KRL, K1, repeat from * to end of round—8 sts.

Round 3: Knit.

Round 4: *KRL, K1, repeat from * to end of round—16 sts.

Round 5: Knit.

Round 6: *K1, M1L, K2, M1R, K1, repeat from * to end of round—24 sts.

Round 7: Knit.

Round 8: *K1, M1L, K4, M1R, K1, repeat from * to end of round—32 sts.

Round 9: Knit.

Round 10: *K1, M1L, K6, M1R, K1, repeat from * to end of round—40 sts.

Rounds 11-17: Knit.

Round 18: *SSK, K16, K2tog, repeat from * to end of round—36 sts.

Round 19: Knit.

Round 20: *SSK, K14, K2tog, repeat from * to end of round—32 sts.

Round 21: Knit.

Round 22: *SSK, K12, K2tog, repeat from * to end of round—28 sts.

Round 23: Knit.

Round 24: *SSK, K10, K2tog, repeat from * to end of round—24 sts.

Round 25: Knit.

Round 26: *SSK, K8, K2tog, repeat from * to end of round—20 sts.

Round 27: Knit.

If working with dpns, transfer half of sts to one needle. If working with two circular needles, half of sts will already be on one needle, making this step unnecessary. Either way, the next section is worked back and forth using just half the round of sts.

Shape the head by working short rows in the following manner:

Row 1: K9, w&t.

Row 2: P8, w&t.

Row 3: K1, M1R, K2, M1R, K2, M1L, K2, M1L, w&t.

Row 4: P10, w&t.

Row 5: K1, M1R, K3, M1R, K2, M1L, K3, M1L, w&t.

Row 6: P12, w&t.

Row 7: K1, M1R, K4, M1R, K2, M1L, K4, M1L, w&t.

Row 8: P14, w&t.

Row 9: K15, w&t.

Row 10: P16, w&t.

Row 11: K17, w&t.

Row 12: P18, w&t.

Row 13: K5, SSK, K4, K2tog, K6, w&t.

Row 14: P18, w&t.

Complete the head by switching from short rows to rounds:

Round 28: K6, SSK, K2, K2tog, K7. Before working the first st, pick up a couple of the wraps from the junction between the short row section and the rest of the round. Knit these together with the next st (this is not an increase, just a measure to prevent holes from forming between the short row section and the rest of the round). K to end of round.

Round 29: Before working the first st, pick up a couple of the wraps from the junction between the short row section and the rest of the round. Knit these together with the first st. Continue as follows: K6, SSK, K2tog, K to end of round.

Round 30: K7, K2tog, K to end of round. BO all sts.

Arm Assembly

Pick up 3 sts in MC from the top selvedge of each arm for a total of 24 sts, as shown in Figure 1. Join in a round.

Figure 1

Rounds 1–3: Knit.

Round 4: K12, M1R, K12—25 sts.

BO all 25 sts.

Close the base of the arm assembly as follows. Turn the arm assembly upside down. In CC, pick up 40 sts from the underside of the arm assembly as shown in Figure 2.

Figure 2

Take extra care when picking up sts at the regions where the tentacles intersect, as holes can easily form in these areas. To prevent this, be sure to pick up 2 sts at each intersection point, one on each side of the middle st.

Join these 40 sts into a round and proceed in CC as follows:

Rounds 1–3: Knit.

Round 4: *K2tog, repeat from * to end of round—20 sts.

Round 5: Knit.

Round 6: *K2tog, repeat from * to end of round—10 sts.

Round 7: *K2tog, repeat from * to end—5 sts. Cut yarn and thread through remaining sts. Pull tight. The underside of your assembly should now resemble Figure 3.

Figure 3

Fold eight chenille stems in half and twist tightly. The folded chenille stems will have one blunt end (the folded end) and one sharp end. Carefully insert one folded chenille stem into each tentacle, blunt end first. When finished, all the sharp ends will be pointing toward the center of the assembly. Fold each chenille stem upward and twist all eight around each other as in Figure 4. Wrap with generous quantities of waste yarn until there are no more protruding sharp ends.

Figure 4

Finishing

Using bits of light and dark colored yarn, embroider eyes onto the head. Lightly stuff the head and mantle with fiberfill. Graft the tentacle assembly onto the head and mantle using fake grafting techniques. Weave in any loose ends with a tapestry needle.

Jellyfish

Jellyfish are beautiful, but potentially painful denizens of the sea. Luckily, this knit version is lovely, but lacks nematocysts. A relatively easy project, it will give you great practice with working simultaneously in multiple colors (stranded knitting), knitting in the round, and picking up stitches.

yarn
Worsted weight
MC (rose): 30 yd (27.5 m)
CC1 (gray): 30 yd (27.5 m)
CC2 (pink): 50 yd (46 m)

needles
• One set U.S. size 5 (3.75 mm) double-pointed needles
and/or
• Two U.S. size 5 (3.75 mm) circular needles,
24" (61 cm) long

notions
• Fiberfill stuffing
• Tapestry needle

gauge
22 to 24 sts = 4" (10 cm) in stockinette stitch

dimensions
Bell diameter: 4" (10 cm)
Oral arm length: 10" to 20"
(25.5 to 51 cm)

difficulty
Beginner/Intermediate

Pattern

Bell

In CC1, CO 4 sts. Join these sts into a round, and proceed:
Round 1: K-fb 4 times—8 sts.
Round 2: Knit.
Rounds 3–24: Follow chart. Note that for each round, you will be repeating the chart 8 times.

Chart

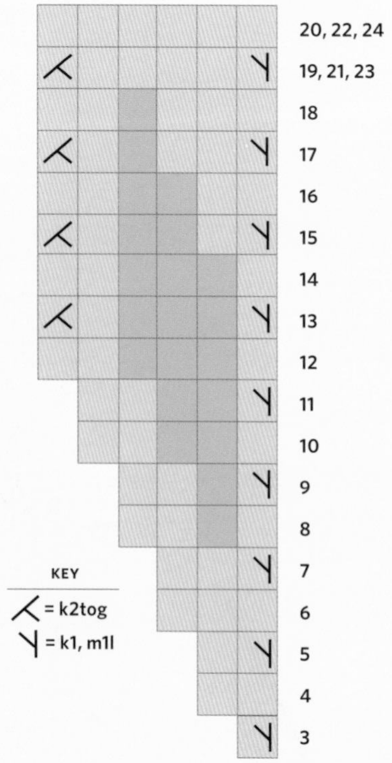
20, 22, 24
19, 21, 23
18
17
16
15
14
13
12
11
10
9
8
7
6
5
4
3
KEY
= k2tog
= k1, m1l

Round 25: *K1, KLL, repeat from * to end of round—96 sts.

BO all sts as follows: *turn work and CO 3 sts using the cable CO method, BO 6 sts, repeat from * until all sts are bound off.

Underside of Bell

Turn work over. In MC, pick up 48 sts approximately 1" (2.5 cm) from the edge of the bell.

See **Figure 1** for guidance.

Figure 1

Join these sts into a round and continue:

Rounds 1–3: Knit.

Round 4: *K2tog, repeat from * to end of round—24 sts.

Round 5: Knit.

Round 6: *K2tog, repeat from * to end of round—12 sts.

Round 7: *K2tog, repeat from * to end of round—6 sts.

Stuff the bell with fiberfill. Do not overstuff! Cut yarn, thread through final 6 sts, and pull tight.

Oral Arms

You will be making 4 oral arms for your jelly.

To make the first arm, CO 35 sts in CC2 using the knit-on method. Continue, working back and forth in rows, as follows:

Row 1: [K-tbl, YO] 16 times, K-tbl 3 times, [YO, K-tbl] 16 times—67 sts.

Row 2: Sl1, K32, w&t.

Row 3: [K1, YO] 15 times, K-tbl 3 times, [YO, K1] 15 times—97 sts.

Row 4: Sl1, K30, w&t.

Row 5: [K1, YO] 30 times, K1—127 sts.

BO all sts. Cut yarn, thread through final lp, and pull tight.

To make the second arm, CO 51 sts in CC2 using the knit-on method. Continue, working back and forth in rows, as follows:

Row 1: [K-tbl, YO] 24 times, K-tbl 3 times, [YO, K-tbl] 24 times—99 sts.

Row 2: Sl1, K48, w&t.

Row 3: [K1, YO] 23 times, K-tbl 3 times, [YO, K1] 23 times—145 sts.

Row 4: Sl1, K46, w&t.

Row 5: [K1, YO] 46 times, K1—191 sts.

BO all sts. Cut yarn, thread through final lp, and pull tight.

To make the third oral arm, CO 65 sts in CC2 using the knit-on method. Continue, working back and forth in rows, as follows:

Row 1: [K-tbl, YO] 31 times, K-tbl 3 times, [YO, K-tbl] 31 times—127 sts.

Row 2: Sl1, K62, w&t.

Row 3: [K1, YO] 30 times, K-tbl 3 times, [YO, K1] 30 times—187 sts.

Row 4: Sl1, K60, w&t.

Row 5: [K1, YO] 60 times, K1—247 sts.

BO all sts. Cut yarn, thread through final lp, and pull tight.

To make the fourth oral arm, CO 99 sts in CC2 using the knit-on method. Continue, working back and forth in rows, as follows:

Row 1: [K-tbl, YO] 48 times, K-tbl 3 times, [YO, K-tbl] 48 times—195 sts.

Row 2: Sl1, K96, w&t.

Row 3: [K1, YO] 47 times, K-tbl 3 times, [YO, K1] 47 times—289 sts.

Row 4: Sl1, K94, w&t.

Row 5: [K1, YO] 94 times, K1—383 sts.
BO all sts. Cut yarn, thread through final lp, and pull tight.

Stinging Tentacles

Cut a 9" and 15" (23 to 38 cm) length of CC1 yarn. Carefully separate the plies in each of these lengths to get several single-ply pieces. Attach these single-ply lengths to the edges of the bell.

Finishing

Attach the oral arms to the underside of the bell. Take care of any loose yarn ends.

Black-Devil Anglerfish

The mating behavior of the deep-sea anglerfish is probably one of the most bizarre in the entire animal kingdom. Because locating a mate is a difficult affair in the sparsely populated deep ocean, a male who meets a female can't afford to let her get away. Being only one-tenth of her size, he attaches himself to her with his sharp teeth. Over time, his circulation fuses with hers, and he becomes a part of her, providing a lifetime supply of sperm for the pair's reproductive needs.

Depending on your tastes, you may knit this design with or without the parasitic male angler. Either way, this is a fun, quirky knit!

yarn
Worsted weight
MC (dark gray): 30 yd (27.5 m)
CC1 (light gary): 30 yd (27.5 m)
CC2 (navy): 25 yd (23 m)

needles
- One set U.S. size 5 (3.75 mm) double-pointed needles
and/or
- Two U.S. size 5 (3.75 mm) circular needles, 24" (61 cm) long
- Stitch holder

notions
- Fiberfill stuffing
- Tapestry needle
- One 12" (30.5 cm) chenille stem (optional)

gauge
22 to 24 sts = 4" (10 cm) in stockinette stitch

dimensions
Length: 8" (20 cm)
Height: 4" (10 cm)

difficulty
Intermediate/ Experienced

Pattern

Dorsum (Upper Side)

In MC, CO 8 sts. Continue, working back and forth in rows:

Row 1: Sl1, P6, K1.

Row 2: Sl1, K2, M1R, K2, M1L, K3—10 sts.

Row 3: Sl1, P8, K1.

Row 4: Sl1, K3, M1R, K2, M1L, K4—12 sts.

Row 5: Sl1, P10, K1.

Row 6: Sl1, K4, M1R, K2, M1L, K5—14 sts.

Row 7: Sl1, P12, K1.

Row 8: Sl1, K5, M1R, K2, M1L, K6—16 sts.

Row 9: Sl1, P14, K1.

Row 10: Sl1, K6, M1R, K2, M1L, K7—18 sts.

Row 11: Sl1, P16, K1.

Row 12: Sl1, K7, M1R, K2, M1L, K8—20 sts.

Row 13: Sl1, P18, K1.

Row 14: Sl1, K8, M1R, K2, M1L, K9—22 sts.

Row 15: Sl1, P20, K1.

Row 16: Sl1, K9, M1R, K2, M1L, K10—24 sts.

Row 17: Sl1, P22, K1.

Row 18: Sl1, K10, M1R, K2, M1L, K11—26 sts.

Row 19: Sl1, P24, K1.

Row 20: Sl1, K11, M1R, K2, M1L, K12—28 sts.

Row 21: Sl1, P26, K1.

Row 22: Sl1, K12, M1R, K2, M1L, K13—30 sts.

Row 23: Sl1, P28, K1.

Row 24: Sl1, K13, M1R, K2, M1L, K14—32 sts.

Row 25: Sl1, P30, K1.

Row 26: Sl1, K14, M1R, K2, M1L, K15—34 sts.

Row 27: Sl1, P32, K1.

Row 28: Sl1, K15, M1R, K2, M1L, K16—36 sts.

Row 29: Sl1, P34, K1.

Row 30: Sl1, K16, M1R, K2, M1L, K17—38 sts.

Row 31: Sl1, P36, K1.

Row 32: Sl1, K17, M1R, K2, M1L, K18—40 sts.

Row 33: Sl1, P38, K1.

Row 34: Sl1, K27, w&t.

Row 35: P16, w&t.

Row 36: K3, SSK, K6, K2tog, K7, w&t—38 sts.

Row 37: P22, w&t.

Row 38: K7, SSK, K4, K2tog, K11, w&t—36 sts.

Row 39: P28, w&t.

Row 40: K11, SSK, K2, K2tog, K15, w&t—34 sts.

Row 41: Sl1, P32, K1.

BO all sts.

Belly (Lower Side)

Use MC yarn and pick up 28 sts kwise along the selvedge of the work, beginning at the tail region and moving toward the head. Continue working in rows as follows:

Row 1: P10, w&t.

Row 2: K6, [M1R, K1] 3 times, P1—31 sts.

Row 3: Sl1, P15, w&t.

Row 4: K9, [K1, M1R, K1] 3 times, P1—34 sts.

Row 5: Sl1, P21, w&t.

Row 6: K12, [K2, M1R, K1] 3 times, P1—37 sts.

Row 7: Sl1, P27, w&t.

Row 8: K15, [K3, M1R, K1] 3 times, P1—40 sts.

Row 9: Sl1, P33, w&t.

Row 10: K18, [K4, M1R, K1] 3 times, P1—43 sts.

Row 11: Sl1, P39, w&t.

Row 12: K21, [K5, M1R, K1] 3 times, P1—46 sts.

Row 13: Sl1, P45.

Row 14: K24, [K6, M1R, K1] 3 times, P1—49 sts.

Row 15: Sl1, P48.

Cut MC yarn, and place 49 sts on a holder. Turn work, and pick up another 28 sts kwise from the opposite selvedge of the work, beginning at the head region and traveling toward the tail. Continue working in rows as follows:

Row 1: P28.

Row 2: Sl1, [K1, M1L] 3 times, K6, w&t—31 sts.

Row 3: P13.

Row 4: Sl1, [K1, M1L, K1] 3 times, K9, w&t—34 sts.

Row 5: P19.

Row 6: Sl1, [K1, M1L, K2] 3 times, K12, w&t—37 sts.

Row 7: P25.

Row 8: Sl1, [K1, M1L, K3] 3 times, K15, w&t—40 sts.

Row 9: P31.

Row 10: Sl1, [K1, M1L, K4] 3 times, K18, w&t—43 sts.

Row 11: P37.

Row 12: Sl1, [K1, M1L, K5] 3 times, K21, w&t—46 sts.

Row 13: P43.

Row 14: Sl1, [K1, M1L, K6] 3 times, K23, P1—49 sts.

Row 15: Sl1, P48.

Row 16: Sl1, K47, P1.

Row 17: Sl1, P48.

Cut MC yarn, leaving a long tail. Using this long yarn tail and a tapestry needle, graft (Kitchener stitch) the 49 sts from the first needle to the 49 sts on the second needle.

Upper Lip

Using CC1, pick up 34 sts from the BO edge of the dorsum. Work these sts as follows:

Row 1: P33, K1.

Row 2: Sl1, K33.

Row 3: Sl1, P32, K1.

Row 4: Sl1, K33.

Row 5: Sl1, P29, w&t.

Row 6: K26, w&t.

Row 7: P22, w&t.

Row 8: K18, w&t.

Row 9: P25, K1.

BO all sts. Cut CC1 yarn, leaving a long tail. Using long tail of yarn and a tapestry needle, fold the lip up and whip st the BO edge to the upper edge where you picked up the sts initially.

Lower Lip

Using CC1, pick up 30 sts from the selvedge on the bottom of the jaw. Continue working these sts as follows:

Row 1: Sl1, P28, K1.

Row 2: Sl1, K29.

Row 3: Sl1, P28, K1.

Row 4: Sl1, K29.

Row 5: Sl1, P25, w&t.

Row 6: K10, M1R, K2, M1L, K10, w&t.

Row 7: P20, w&t.

Row 8: K7, M1R, K2, M1L, K7, w&t.

Row 9: P14, w&t.

Row 10: K10, w&t.

Row 11: P16, w&t.

Row 12: K9, K2tog, SSK, K9, w&t.

Row 13: P25, K1.

Row 14: Sl1, K12, K2tog, SSK, K13.

BO all sts. Cut CC1 yarn, leaving a long tail. Using this long yarn tail, whip st the BO edge of the lower lip to the edge of the chin where you originally picked up sts.

Inside of Mouth

Using **Figure 1** as a guide, pick up a total of 27 sts in CC2 yarn on the inside edge of the lower lip.

Figure 1

Continue, working in rows, as follows:

Row 1: Sl1, P24, w&t.

Row 2: K23, w&t.

Row 3: P21, w&t.

Row 4: K19, w&t.

Row 5: P17, w&t.

Row 6: K15, w&t.

Row 7: P14, w&t.

Row 8: K13, w&t.

Row 9: P15, w&t.

Row 10: K17, w&t.

Row 11: P19, w&t.

Row 12: K21, w&t.

Row 13: P23, K1.

Row 14: Sl1, K26.

BO all sts.

Stuff the body of the fish with fiberfill, being careful not to overstuff.

Cut CC3 yarn, leaving a long tail. Using a tapestry needle and this long tail, whip st this BO edge to the inner edge of the upper lip.

Tail Fin

Use MC yarn, and beginning from the midline of the back, pick up 10 sts along the open end of the tail region. Turn the work, and pick up an additional 10 sts along the other side of the opening for a total of 20 sts. Use **Figure 2** as a guide to the placement of these sts.

Figure 2

Join these sts into a round and continue:

Rounds 1 & 2: Knit.

Round 3: [K1, M1L, K3, M1R, K1] 4 times— 28 sts.

Cut MC yarn, and switch to CC1. Continue:

Rounds 4–9: [K1, P1, K1, P1, K1, P1, K1] 4 times.

Round 10: [SSK, K1, P1, K1, P1, K2, P1, K1, P1, K1, K2tog] 2 times—24 sts.

Round 11: [K2, P1, K1, P1, K2, P1, K1, P1, K2] 2 times.

Round 12: [SSK, P1, K1, P1, K2, P1, K1, P1, K2tog] 2 times—20 sts.

Round 13: [K1, P1, K1, P1, K1] 4 times.

Cut yarn, leaving a long tail. Divide the 20 sts evenly between two needles. Using your tapestry needle, graft (Kitchener st) the sts on the first needle to the sts on the second needle.

Dorsal Fin

Using CC1 yarn, pick up 15 sts along the midline of the back near the tail fin. When picking up these sts, begin at the tail region and continue along the midline of the back toward the head region. Turn the work, and, using a new needle, pick up another 15 sts directly behind the first 15 sts. Use **Figure 3** as a guide to the placement of these sts.

Figure 3

Join these 30 sts into a round and continue:

Round 1: *[K1, P1] 7 times, K1, repeat from * to end of round.

Round 2: SSK, [K1, P1] 6 times, K2, [P1, K1] 6 times, K2tog—28 sts.

Round 3: SSK, [P1, K1] 6 times, [K1, P1] 6 times, K2tog—26 sts.

Round 4: SSK, [K1, P1] 5 times, K2, [P1, K1] 5 times, K2tog—24 sts.

Round 5: SSK, [P1, K1] 5 times, [K1, P1] 5 times, K2tog—22 sts.

Round 6: SSK, [K1, P1] 3 times, K1, K2tog, SSK, K1, [P1, K1] 3 times, K2tog—18 sts.

Cut yarn, leaving a long tail. Divide 18 sts evenly onto two needles and, using a tapestry needle, graft (Kitchener st) the sts from the first needle to the sts on the second needle.

Pectoral Fins

Using MC yarn, pick up 6 sts along the side of the body. Turn work and pick up another 6 sts directly behind the first 6 sts. Use **Figure 4** as a guide to the placement of these sts.

Figure 4

Join these 12 sts into a round and continue:

Rounds 1 & 2: Knit.

Round 3: [K1, M1L, K1, M1R, K1] 4 times—20 sts.

Cut MC yarn, and attach CC1 yarn. Continue:

Rounds 4–8: [K1, P1, K1, P1, K1] 4 times.

Round 9: *SSK, [K1, P1, K1] 2 times, K2tog, repeat from * to end of round—16 sts.

Round 10: [K2, P1, K2, P1, K2] 2 times.

Round 11: [SSK, P1, K2, P1, K2tog] 2 times—12 sts.

Round 12: [K1, P1, K1] 4 times.

Cut yarn, leaving a long tail. Divide 12 sts evenly onto two needles. Using a tapestry needle, graft (Kitchener st) the sts from the first needle to the sts on the second needle.

Work the opposite pectoral fin by picking up 12 sts on the opposite side of the body and working identically.

Teeth *(Make 4)*

In CC3, CO 4 sts. Work seven rows of I-cord. Work three more rows as follows, continuing to work as I-cord:

Row 1: K2tog, K2.

Row 2: K3.

Row 3: K2tog, K1.

Cut yarn, thread through remaining two sts, and pull tight.

Lure

In MC, CO 30 sts. Continue, working back and forth in rows:

Row 1: Sl1, P29.

Row 2: Sl1, K4, w&t.

Row 3: P5.

Row 4: Sl1, K28, P1.

Row 5: Sl1, P3, w&t.

Row 6: K3, P1.

Row 7: Sl1, P29.

Row 8: Sl1, K4, w&t.

Row 9: P5.

Row 10: Sl1, K28, P1.

Continuing with MC yarn, turn the work, and using a second needle, pick up another 30 sts from the CO edge of the work. Cut MC yarn, leaving a long tail. Using this long yarn tail and a tapestry needle, graft (Kitchener st) the 30 sts on the original needle to the 30 sts on the second needle.

Now, use CC1 to pick up 8 sts around the circumference of the smaller end of the tube. Join these 8 sts in a round and continue:

Rounds 1–2: Knit.

Cut CC1 yarn, and attach CC3 to work. Continue:

Round 3: [K1, KLL, KRL, K1] 4 times—16 sts.

Round 4: Knit.

Round 5: [K1, M1L, K2, M1R, K1] 4 times— 24 sts.

Rounds 6–8: Knit.

Round 9: [SSK, K8, K2tog] 2 times—20 sts.

Round 10: Knit.

Round 11: [SSK, K6, K2tog] 2 times—16 sts.

Round 12: Knit.

Round 13: [SSK, K4, K2tog] 2 times—12 sts.

Round 14: [SSK, K2, K2tog] 2 times—8 sts.

Cut CC3 yarn, leaving a long tail. Stuff the tip of the lure with fiberfill.

Divide remaining 8 sts evenly onto two needles. Using long yarn tail and tapestry needle, graft (Kitchener st) the sts on the first needle to the sts on the second needle.

Parasitic Male *(Optional)*

You may position the parasitic male anywhere on the body of the female angler. Use MC to pick up 4 sts in desired location. Turn the work and pick up another 4 sts behind the first 4 sts. Join these 8 sts into a round and continue:

Round 1: Knit.

Round 2: [K1, M1L, K2, M1L, K1] 2 times—12 sts.

Rounds 3–7: Knit.

Round 8: [SSK, K2, K2tog] 2 times—8 sts.

Stuff the body of the male with fiberfill. Continue:

Round 9: [SSK, K2tog] 2 times—4 sts.

Round 10: Knit.

Round 11: [K1, KLL, KRL, K1] 2 times—8 sts.

Switch to CC1 and continue.

Rounds 12: [K1, P2, K1] 2 times.

Round 13: [K1, P1, KLL, KRL, P1, K1] 2 times— 12 sts.

Rounds 14–15: [K1, P1, K1] 4 times.

Cut yarn, leaving a long tail. Divide 12 sts evenly onto two needles. Using long yarn tail, graft (Kitchener st) the sts on the first needle to the sts on the second needle.

Finishing

If desired, fold a chenille stem in half, tightly twist it, and insert it into the lure. Attach (mattress st) the lure to the midline of the forehead. Use CC3 yarn to embroider eyes onto the head of the angler. Embroider eyes onto the parasitic male (if applicable). Attach the four teeth to the inside of the mouth.

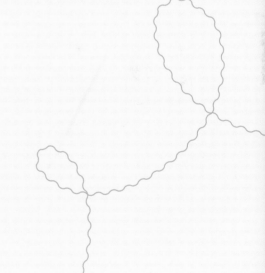

Sea Star

This lovely little echinoderm is quick and easy, a great knit for those times when you're seeking some instant gratification. It will also help you practice decreases, short rows, and picking up stitches. Make an entire collection in varying yarn weights and colors for a real plush treat!

yarn
Worsted weight
MC (purple/blue): 40 yd (36.5 m)
CC (taupe): 40 yd (36.5 m)

needles
• One set U.S. size 5 (3.75 mm) double-pointed needles
and/or
• Two U.S. size 5 (3.75 mm) circular needles,
24" (61 cm) long

notions
• Fiberfill stuffing
• Tapestry needle

gauge
22 to 24 sts = 4" (10 cm) in stockinette stitch

dimensions
Diameter: 8" (20 cm)

difficulty
Beginner/Intermediate

Pattern

Arms (Make 5)

In MC, CO 15 sts. Continue working back and forth in rows as follows:

Row 1: Sl1, P13, K1.

Row 2: Sl1, K5, Sl2-K1-P2SSO, K6—13 sts.

Rows 3 & 5: Sl1, P11, K1.

Row 4: Sl1, K12.

Row 6: Sl1, K4, Sl2-K1-P2SSO, K5—11 sts.

Rows 7 & 9: Sl1, P9, K1.

Row 8: Sl1, K10.

Row 10: Sl1, K3, Sl2-K1-P2SSO, K4—9 sts.

Rows 11 & 13: Sl1, P7, K1.

Row 12: Sl1, K8.

Row 14: Sl1, K2, Sl2-K1-P2SSO, K3—7 sts.

Rows 15 & 17: Sl1, P5, K1.

Row 16: Sl1, K6.

Row 18: Sl1, K1, Sl2-K1-P2SSO, K2—5 sts.

Rows 19 & 21: Sl1, P3, K1.

Row 20: Sl1, K4.

Row 22: Sl1, Sl2-K1-P2SSO, K1—3 sts.

Row 23: Sl2-P1-P2SSO—1 st.

Cut yarn, thread through final st and pull tight. Beginning from the base of the arm and ending at the tip, use CC and pick up 12 sts from the selvedge of the arm. You will be picking these sts up kwise from the right side of the work at a rate of 1 st per two rows. Turn the work. Beginning at the tip and ending at the base of the arm, pick up another 12 sts from the other selvedge of the arm. Once again, you will be picking these sts up kwise from the right side of the work at a rate of 1 st per two rows. See **Figure 1** for guidance. You should now have a total of 24 sts.

Figure 1

Continue, working back and forth in rows, as follows:

Row 1 (wrong side): Sl1, K7, w&t.

Row 2: P8.

Row 3: Sl1, K3, w&t.

Row 4: P4.

Row 5: Sl1, K10, P2tog-tbls, P2tog, K10, P1—24 sts.

Row 6: Sl1, P5, w&t.

Row 7: K5, P1.

Row 8: Sl1, P9, K1.

Divide 24 sts evenly onto two needles. Using the three-needle BO method, BO all sts. Cut yarn, thread through final st and pull tight.

Assembly of Arms

In MC, pick up 8 sts from the CO edge of each of the five arms for a total of 40 sts. See **Figure 2** for guidance.

Join these sts into a round and proceed:

Round 1: Knit.

Round 2: *K6, K2tog, repeat from * to end of round—35 sts.

Round 3: *K5, K2tog, repeat from * to end of round—30 sts.

Round 4: *K4, K2tog, repeat from * to end of round—25 sts.

Round 5: *K3, K2tog, repeat from * to end of round—20 sts.

Round 6: *K2, K2tog, repeat from * to end of round—15 sts.

Round 7: *K1, K2tog, repeat from * to end of round—10 sts.

Round 8: *K2tog, repeat from * to end of round—5 sts.

Cut yarn, thread through final 5 sts and pull tight.

Figure 2

Figure 3

Underside

Turn the work over. Using CC yarn, pick up a total of 70 sts around the open underside of the sea star. Pick up these sts as follows: 6 sts in between each of the arms and 8 sts on the CC selvedge of the underside of each arm. See **Figure 3** for guidance in picking up these sts. Join these 70 sts into a round and continue:

Rounds 1–3: Knit.

Round 4: *K2tog 17 times, K1, repeat from * to end of round—36 sts.

Round 5: Knit.

Round 6: *K2tog, repeat from * to end of round—18 sts.

Carefully stuff the arms of the sea star and the central body region with fiberfill. Do not overstuff! Continue:

Round 7: *K2tog 4 times, K1, repeat from * to end of round—10 sts.

Round 8: *K2tog 2 times, K1, repeat from * to end of round—6 sts.

Cut yarn, thread through final 6 sts and pull tight.

Finishing

Take care of any loose yarn ends.

Sun Star

Sun stars are among the most voracious invertebrate predators, which is one reason that many undersea enthusiasts don't include them in home aquariums. This knit sun star, on the other hand, will make a lovely addition to your undersea collection, and you don't need to worry about its appetite at all! It also provides great practice with short rows, picking up stitches, and knitting in the round.

yarn
Worsted weight
MC (orange): 60 yd (55 m)
CC (yellow): 30 yd (27.5 m)

needles
· One set U.S. size 5 (3.75 mm) double-pointed needles
and/or
· Two U.S. size 5 (3.75 mm) circular needles, 24" (61 cm) long

notions
· Fiberfill stuffing
· Tapestry needle

gauge
22 to 24 sts = 4" (10 cm) in stockinette stitch

dimensions
Diameter: 10" (25.5 cm)

difficulty
Beginner/Intermediate